DESTINED TO BE HANGED

The Epic Story of
the Gentlemen Pirates Who
Pursued the South Seas,
Saved a Princess, and Stole
a Fortune

Ryan A. Red

List of chapters

CHAPTER 1

This book is genuinely awesome. The arrangement of encounters is exquisitely created, all around informed, and especially got a handle on, with gold pieces threw all through and slyly situated. I've skewed the bigger part since the maker's most recent works have been shown to be entirely significant.
Thomson makes history as it should be made, as it ended up actually working, with supporting evidence. Thomson similarly consolidates dates and significant stretches of events, which are uncommon in many annals anytime recorded. This is exceptionally steady similar to giving setting and associating ongoing advancements for the peruser. As the story pours forward total real factors and records of the appropriating privateers journeys and people they meet, this is the spine from which the wide range of various things exude. The additional history is thrown all through, adding to the arrangement of encounters' splendor. I like how he relates current things to events in the last piece of the 1600s.

The text is uncommonly particular and sharp. There are more than two or three essayists that make history as a work of fiction. This is on a very basic level better compared to that. Between what may be dull history and imaginative talk to work on the storyline, the creating shimmers.

Thomson deftly twists around together recorded undeniable points of view into a persuading show that keeps you expecting to understand more. It's the mystery of who lives where, additionally, how in this current situation. It's unquestionably worth perusing, and it's most likely going to stir the interests of individuals who aren't without a doubt, even roused by history or privateers. This is a must-peruse for we who work in the field of history.

All things considered, I unequivocally propose this book. The score is 10 out of ten.

The most un-insane thing that occurs in this novel is a man being marooned on an island for quite a while. In kayaks, the ostensible privateers assault Spanish oceanic boats. They coincidentally wind themselves near the Icy Landmass at one point. It's uncommon that I go over a consistent with life book that is both engaging and very much educated. I simply wish there weren't almost as many names to remember.

Who doesn't see the worth in validity that doesn't peruse like consistent with life. I'm remaining here!

I've been getting a lot of books actually that are stacked with information, experience, fast moving, perusing, and attracting storylines. One more to add to the overview is Born to Be Hanged. Privateers and the times in which they lived have long excited my interest. Out on the wide seas, spreading commotion and causing a ruckus any spot they go... indeed, that is my direction. With this one, I completely got that, as well as essentially more.

I acquired some valuable information more about being a privateer than I had as of late perceived, particularly the way that English Pirates battled with the Spaniards. This is obviously for book dears, yet I would propose it to anybody with any interest whatsoever in more profoundly concentrating on this season of history. Treasure, savage battles, a caught princess, and many encounters are the thing I'm alluding to. It's a lot of bliss to peruse.

Creator Keith Thomson turns a hypnotizing genuine story of English privateers, loot, a princess, and tirelessness even with unlimited possibilities and hazardous conditions. Thompson's dynamic style whisks us away to the seventeenth hundred years.
We travel with them along South America's Pacific coast, which was once Spain's property and England's adversary. The creator's investigation is noteworthy, and he uses the privateers' contemporaneous journals and verification.

This book gives the peruser a unique investigate the presence of these difficult privateers as they get rival boats, seek after immense fortunes, and safeguard their country's benefits as they sail out of the Caribbean.

Their words give us a short investigate their reality as they venture the seas, face clashes, leave on perilous trips, and search for value from the most critical maritime court. It is both a staggering excursion and a basic book. It was surely a five-star understanding.

This is a fascinating investigate what burglary looked like in the South Oceans, following one get-together's turn of events and obliteration. It has a tendency to go wrong while focusing on no unquestionable last arrangement (the Princess gets saved without skipping a beat, and subsequently it's basically erratic assault later assault), and I felt like it was lacking concerning some sort by and large. For what reason were these privateers picked as the legends of the record rather than others? What was the sign of this book? Is this a show about how piratrs looked when in doubt, or are these characters remarkable?

I favored it, but I wish there had been a more prominent measure of a central subject to completely finish all the story. This was heaps of entertaining to peruse. These individuals went with the decision to transform into privateers in the South Pacific. They burglarized the Spanish, who were busy with rapping the new globe, of millions of dollars. The diarists who were with the privateers are positive in the book. The way that these records make me shocked has been expected for pretty much 300 years. Being a privateer during the Brilliant Period of Robbery is apparently heaps of horseplay, in Errol Flynn or Disney's motion pictures. Call yourself marauders, your mates privateers, and you'll get letters of marque to go after adversary's boats, grab their abundance, sail away, and go through the late night praising with your amigos.

CHAPTER 2

Destined to Be Hanged: This book depicts the sensational story of the good men Pirate who struck the South Oceans, saved a Princess, likewise, Took a Fortune by Keith Thomson uncovers an entirely unexpected reality. A privateer needed to endeavor to disturb the foe, journeying colossal distances with deficient food, broken boats, and a portion of the time untrustworthy association.
The book opens with a short layout of the period and the many powers that dealt with the region, including Spanish, English, and French. With contemplations of loot, a bunch of different individuals from everywhere Europe and all gatherings of companions join in the Caribbean.

To free a close by princess and their store from the Spanish, the men gather as one and go overland to a little town.

They are compelling in their attack yet find that the overflow has been moved to security. Not satisfied with this, the officials headed out again through Panama, going through rainforest and roaring streams until they showed up at the South Ocean, where they shipped off an attack on networks the whole way across the Pacific.

There are fortunes to be secured, property to be destroyed, and lives to be lost. A few people become exhausted of life and return to Britain, where they are sought after for their bad behaviors. Some leave and obscure into absence of definition. Furthermore, a re-appearance of the fundamental life they've ever known.

The book is extraordinarily perused and streams like a novel while telling an enamoring and cautious history of the time frame. A ton of the information in the book comes from the privateers' own words, diaries, court records, and, shockingly, a book or a transformed two formed by a privateer into a maker. There is a care that bits of the narratives are designed, particularly during a fundamental, or are stacked with gloats and deceptions while chatting with the people, yet at the same time the overall story may be given. That's what my primary thing is, regardless, when things could have gone all the more effectively, the privateers for the most part pick the more problematic way.

Seizures, sea fights, life prepared, and a lot of walking and cruising have a lot of this story. There was a lot of cruising. My super significant issue was that there were different privateers conveying their records, and it was as often as possible testing to perceive who was who. That, in any case, was a minor issue. A combination of swashes and catches.

This is a colossal book to give as a Dad's Day present or to peruse around the sea. Admirers of history, and Pirates fans will like this book. Furthermore, for the people who have seen the film episode about privateer ships, and for fans like me, who used to go through quite a while playing Syd Meier's Pirate game.

This sumptuously bare essential book delivers the peruser to the Caribbean, where they may be seen paddling in kayaks, scouring Spanish vessel transports, and searching for food on remote locations searching for gold and silver. The book is richly created, with a mix of journal entries and assessment to completely investigate what life looked like for these people who traveled all through the South Pacific in journey for overflow.

There's an extraordinary arrangement to like in this book since it's stacked up with real stories. The book should be acknowledged with some aversion since the people might have extended their records, as they were regularly inebriated, unwell, and doing combating for their lives. Investigating the streams was never clear, even with weapons and coarseness, since there were reliably enemies hiding away not excessively far off. Storms were similarly a reliable risk, and when they struck, they could without a very remarkable stretch obliterate a boat or prompt boats to spurn their course, never to be seen again.

For sure, even with a trailblazer, every one of the men in the association expected to make decisions since missions were reliably unsafe and men would unexpectedly leave them. Men were killed in fights, and authority should be changed, so existence unbounded.

This book takes us inside the heads of trying privateers, with a great deal of action. Pieces of information are not found in many books.
This was an intriguing book to peruse! Honestly, I esteemed the subject and took in an exceptional course of action that I didn't know anything about before perusing this book. I've been searching for a beguiling obvious book on privateers since I haven't perused any as of now.

Destined to be Hanged more than met that essential. I was first pulled in by the title then, cover.

This was all around educated and created. Keith Thomson, the creator, even explanations from the lips of the privateers and others who went with them, as well as detailed accounts from the period of time. If you like everything nautical, particularly privateers, I firmly recommend this book.

An extraordinary, confirmed record of a pivotal encounter that persevered through over two years. The most edifying were all of our pirater inclinations, which were completely uncovered.

The novel is stacked with troubling scenes, conflicts, and unequivocal information that keep it associated while furthermore being educational.

CHAPTER 3

Keith Thomson, in this novel, Born to be Hanged, raises seventeenth century stealing to another level. His accentuation is on a band of stable English privateers whose undertakings in the South Oceans went from shielding a close by princess to catching Spanish boats and crushing Spanish posts and towns from Panama to the Isla Duque de York.
The book begins with a remarkable history of burglary in the last piece of the 1600s, showing that the various depictions of striking privateers in current composing don't really reflect the reality of such people.

Thomson centers around a specific social occasion of privateers whose diaries make the tone for the record of their various encounters. Basil Ringrose, a first-time privateer, and skilled mathematician and pilot; Lionel Wafer, a privateer trained professional; Bartholomew Sharp, a privateer captain; William Dampier, a first rate naturalist; New Englander John Cox; Edward Povey, and However, brit whose abilities to create, lacking, would be adequate to keep him from the platform; and William Dick, the most Chief Richard Sawkins, renowned as much for his loot of the Spanish regarding his near escapes from the English, Commander Peter Harris, and the fleet's head of maritime tasks, John Coxon, and Commander Edmond Cooke as chairmen of the mission, are among the maritime privateers named by Thomson.

All of these people was charmed by the possibility of an ocean experience, not to see the chance to fill their wallets with any fortune they could uncover. Additionally, the privateer neighborhood its hands in different spots where those royal gems were prepared for the taking.

An Indian princess is the legend of the story. Her name is dark, but she was seized by Spanish contenders, and her granddad, a Kuna Indian chief, joins the privateers in his yearning to safeguard her. He asks the English privateers for help, promising to help them in investigating through the Panama Channel, unequivocally the Darien Area, close to the South Oceans, where Spanish officials control various islands and metropolitan regions, as well as gold and silver fortune. What might a privateer at some point require more than that?

Thomson cautiously portrays this outing and the princess' rescue, yet there is a vulnerability as for whether she really needed to be saved. Set the energy with intriguing portrayals of islands stacked up with snakes likewise, reptiles. Metropolitan people group where Spanish posts had significant solid areas were made, and the dangers of trips through the land from one sea to one more with negligible in the technique for arrangements, isolated from a couple of the privateers' diaries.

The tensions experienced by the privateers as they seek after their critical goals (cherishes), the expulsion of the Spaniards from their fortresses and boats, run all through the story. Since the story depends on the privateers' journals, the scales are tipped overwhelmingly for the privateers and against the Spanish. It's a thrilling story from begin to finish, whether each exposing succeeds or crashes and burns.

Thomson portrays the larger part rule nature of privateer life, in which decisions are made by a more prominent vote of the privateers rather than by the boss all together. There are various rebellions, as one would anticipate in a tale about privateers. There is a contention between the various sides at a certain point, and the horrendous side is passed on to fight for itself. It's not unexpected to realize about captains getting bound while the gathering searches for another chief to finish the journey. Thomson gives a mind boggling degree of visual truth to the disputes as he portrays the boat's expert's instruments and methods, which habitually incited the lack of limbs, as he depicts the various trips and contacts with the hated Spanish.

Thomson has integrated an aide of the Isthmus of Panama, the South Oceans from the northernmost piece of South America, the Drake Section, and the Straights of Magellan, which lead the privateers back to the Atlantic Sea, the Caribbean Ocean, and at last Britain. As the mission draws in neighboring and the helping through pirates return to Britain to need to manage burglary punishments, there is a tendency that the experience of the underlying 3/4 of the novel has worn off. Regardless, the peruser should not be put off by this. The story is loaded with strain, battle, and unequivocal subtleties, making it both drawing in and educational.

CHAPTER 4

In his book Born to be Hanged, Thomson lifts seventeenth century burglary to another level. The book begins with a spellbinding history of burglary in the last piece of the 1600s, displaying that the various depictions of trying privateers in the current composing are not thoroughly careful depictions of such people. The battles looked by the privateers as they seek after two head goals — loves moreover, the launch of the Spaniards from their posts and ships — run all through the book.

Since the record relies upon the privateers' diaries, the scales are slanted overwhelmingly for the privateers and against the Spanish. Whether each excursion is a victory or a mistake, it's an interesting story start to finish. As the undertaking draws in neighboring and the getting through privateers return to Britain to need to manage burglary punishments, there is a tendency that the experience of the underlying 3/4 of the novel has worn off. In any case, the peruser should not be put off by this.

The novel is stacked up with expectation, battle, likewise, particular real factors, making it both drawing in and instructive.

Thomson portrays the raiders' encounters with uprisings, storms, and risky verdure with mind. Likewise, information, diving into nautical phrasing and burglary customs as he relates the privateers' brushes with disobedience, storms, and deadly plant life.

Thomson adjusts the 'Brethren of the Coast,' uncovering information into their aims, establishments, and relationship by fixating on people who saved accounts of the trip. Specialists of theft and oceanic history will be energized by every movement stuffed page.

Thomson particularly displays Imprint Twain's maxim, Truth is more unusual than fiction. Thomson's privateers burst from the pages as particularly and compellingly as those in the Pirates of the Caribbean film series do on the big screen, because of excited sythesis besides, cautious investigation.

Thomson composes savvy segments that as often as possible completion on a cliffhanger, using high differentiation drawings and advisers for help perusers in following the trips. The creator moreover makes sense of different dull nautical expressions, as aargh, and the starting points of current words like avocado and barbecue.

The elating strain and high power action continue beyond what many would consider possible.

In this book, Thomson unravels the tangled connection point among burglary and boondocks associations in the Americas, where Britain and Spain battle for supreme quality and explore neighborhood social orders, vegetation, besides, regular life in minute detail.
This expedient and connecting with experience of the story will keep perusers locked in.

Destined to Be Hanged peruses like valid fiction and provides the peruser with a reasonable vibe of what the people went through on their unlawful excursion. Removes from these seven diaries are dispersed all through the book, with simply minor changes made to move along the etymological construction and make them more understandable.

These sections from undeniable texts ground what could some way or another radiate an impression of being a work of fiction truth be told... Regardless of how it is centered around adults, Born to Be Hanged is available to young people.

A privateer sweetheart then again an admirer of certain encounters should have a copy in their library, and it is too worth having at home. Destined to Be Hanged is a unique that everyone should peruse.

This was a joy to examine! It was
jam-stacked with captivating real factors and made a reason in certifying or refuting typical convictions and starts about privateers. The stories that were discussed, the consecutive demands in which they were explored, and the basic and responsive tones were all fascinating to me.

I don't peruse a great deal of certified for joy (dangers of being an English and history student — you read an over the top measure of obligatory and research consistent with life to like it in your downtime), yet I participated in this book and the manner by which it dealt with the past through account. I'll doubtlessly be perusing more from Keith Thomson.

I acknowledge the typical difficulty is political opinions getting held up into the story and afterward, by then, beating the peruser with the viewpoints over and over. Accepting the work is presented with political contemplations, I fathom.

Anyway creator was found meandering aimlessly political refuse all through the whole scope of Looney Tunes youngster's shows! I regularly sit before the TV series and dissent exactly when a critical startling advancement occurs.

The chief person sees himself as in an unrealistic situation yet sorts out some way to get through. It has a muddled, delivered vibe about it. What is the relationship among this and Keith Thomson's Born to Be Hanged? For sure, his book is stacked with conditions like this, and the privateers don't all pass on immediately.

Thomson follows the certified story of a band of privateers who set out by strolling across Panama with expectations of freeing a nearby princess and desolating. This trip changes into a two-year odyssey of the most confusing powerful I've anytime perused. While the story is marvelous isolated, Thomson raises the book a lot further. He sees the outlandishness of his character additionally, embraces it. Thomson's sharp asides made me giggle wildly a couple of times. This is an easy to-peruse story that anybody will appreciate.